Life Lessons Learned in 84 Years

Dr. Margaret Mayo Gibson

Margaret Mayo Gibson

AVANTI!

Avanti in Fede Press
Glen Mills, Pennsylvania

The cover shows the author reading to her granddaughter Jenny. Life Lessons start at home.

Acknowledgments

Thanks to Lori Gerber, who inspired me to write *Life Lessons*. Thanks to Winnie Hayek who assembled this book. Thanks to June Bryant, Karen Dickinson, Tom Gibson and Florence Lombardo who gave editorial assistance. Thanks to all my family and friends who helped to teach me these lessons. My wish for readers is to gain insight from these lessons so they too may lead more satisfying lives. AVANTI! GO FORWARD!

CONTENTS

Prologue

I will be forever grateful that Dr. Margaret Mayo Gibson: teacher, guidance counselor, author and dearest friend, agreed to write about her Life Lessons.

Above all her titles, Dr. Gibson is an inspiring, loving mother, grandmother, and great-grandmother to her first great-grandchild, Chase Austin Lane. Her tender, nonjudgmental guidance about parenting and problem solving in general needs to become part of our daily living. Her positive approach enriches our state of mind and empowers us to soul search solutions which enhance our treasured relationships.

She is a dear friend, an inspiration and mentor to me. Dr. Gibson is a true gift to all whose lives she touches.

Lori Gerber

We all respect my mom! 1st row: Grandson Greg, Donna, Mom; 2nd row: Margie (me), Karen, Jeff, Tom.

LESSON 1: ALWAYS RESPECT YOUR ELDERS!

"There is no disputing that the quality of our relationship to our mother is central to our being." **Emily Rosen**

One of my grandchildren asked how many sayings my mom had. Another grandchild answered, "An infinity!" The next question was, "What does that mean?" The reply came quickly. "It never ends!" Indeed, it does seem as though my mom had a saying for every situation in life! Adults during the 1930's & 40's all seemed to have words to live by, words that expressed their family values.

My mother was very caring, especially with the very young and very old. When she insisted I accompany her to see an elderly aunt, I protested. "She is too grouchy! I don't want to visit her." My mother answered, "Be nice to old people, then when you get old, people will be nice to you." Mother chose my middle name after an elderly neighbor who never had children. Mother thought it would be a nice gesture and encouraged me to visit this neighbor often. The problem was that the neighbor did not know how to relate to children. All she ever did when I saw her was to tease me but my mother insisted I visit her often, so I did.

My mother was right. Now that I am elderly, people treat me very well. I'm not sure if it is because people I know are naturally very kind, because I treated elderly people with respect when I was a child, or because the parents of the people who are kind to me also taught them to be nice to the elderly. In the 1930's, if children got in trouble at school, many parents blamed the teachers for being poor instructors. Not my mother! She said, "If you get in trouble at school you will be in double trouble at home!

"Although my mother never had any formal schooling at all, she had definite ideas about appropriate school behavior. "If you sit still and listen to the teacher, you will learn a lot and never get into trouble!" We, my sister, brother and I, had to take the consequences of our actions at home and at school!

One day we visited a friend of my mother's. The friend's grandson was there and proceeded to correct his grandmother's grammar. When we arrived home, my mother said to me, "Never correct an older person's grammar. It does not show respect. Good manners are better than good English!"

LESSON 2: REMEMBER, THERE IS ONE GOD!

"Nothing can dim the light which shines within you." **Maya Angelou**

My mother's father, Vincenzo Borrelli, died from Leukemia when he was 39. My mother's mother, Giovanna, was then 36. At 40, Giovanna married Nicola Pistoia. She became pregnant and gave birth to a girl. Sadly, the baby died in childbirth. It was 1931, the same year I was born. My mother often took me to visit Giovanna for her to hold a baby in her arms. When I was seven years old, I began to visit my grandmother alone. At home I slept in a small bed with my sister. At Giovanna's I had my own room! At home I shared my parents' attention with my sister and younger brother. At Giovanna's house I got all the love and attention from her and my step grandfather Nick. I enjoyed their company!

When I was eight years old, Giovanna said she was buying a white dress with lace, just for me. I was thrilled! She told me I was going to lead her church's procession on the Feast Day August 15. I reminded her that I was not Catholic. She said it was ok because that year she was president of her church's Rosary Society and as her oldest grandchild I would lead the procession. "What will people say?" I asked. She answered confidently. "What can they say? I am following the rule!" "Am I qualified?" I asked. Her response was: "Do you believe in God?" I said I did. "Do you believe in Jesus?" I said I did. "Do you believe Mary is the mother of Jesus?" I said I did. She said, "You are qualified!" I was probably the only Presbyterian in history who ever led a Catholic procession! No one objected. God bless my Grandmother Giovanna for being a truly great role model for me!

Getting ready to process: Grandmom Giovanna and her husband, Cousin Anna, Cousin Louise, Margie (on the right).

LESSON 3: BE GRATEFUL FOR TEACHERS WHO CARE!

"Only a life lived for others is a life worthwhile."
Albert Einstein

In the 1930's, "skipping grades" was a way of accommodating children who were exceptional readers. I started first grade after only a few months in Kindergarten and was skipped from first grade to third grade. The problem was Math. I missed the lessons I needed to handle the Math curriculum. I was told I should just persevere. I continued to excel in Reading and Social Studies. I barely passed Math. I started high school when I was 12 years old. On the first day of Algebra I was not only the youngest student in the class, I was the only one close to tears! After class the teacher asked me to stay. She noticed my distress. I told her I had always had trouble with math and had missed Math lessons when I was skipped. She said, "I will help you. We will find a way for you to spend individual time with me each day until you feel comfortable to do the math on your own. We did it! Or rather, the teacher did it! At the end of the semester I got a B in Algebra! I shall never forget the time and effort Miss Clark gave me. Miss Clark was my role model when I became a teacher.

LESSON 4: MAKE A SPECIAL EFFORT TO GET ALONG WITH FAMILY

"Children need love especially when they don't deserve it." **Harold S. Hubert**

I enjoyed the love and attention I received from my mother's mother, Giovanna. I also learned family values. I was ten and a half months older than my sister. My mother reminded me that I was the older one and I should look after my sister, even though she was much taller and bigger than I.

We slept together in a single bed. My sister Carol and I had different sleep habits and different interests, which understandably caused conflicts! I visited my grandmother Giovanna as often as I could. I loved her and respected her. Unschooled as she was, she taught me valuable lessons in family loyalty! No matter what disagreement my sister and I had, my grandmother would say, "Work it out. She is your sister. She is family."

I grew to love my sister. I miss her daily.

LESSON 5: A PENNY SAVED CAN BRING JOY

"Keep your lives free from the love of money because God will never leave you or forsake you." **Hebrews 13:5**

When I went to high school the carfare was eight cents each way. I was 12 years old and had to take a trolley car and subway to get from Daly Street to Seventeenth and Spring Garden. When it got closer to Christmas, I told my mother I had to leave the house very early to be on time for school. I sure did! I had decided to walk to and from school to save the carfare and spend the money on Christmas presents for my Mom and Dad.

My Mom finally pressed me for details about my early departure for school. I confessed that I was walking forty-five minutes each way to save the carfare. She thought it was too stressful and even dangerous. When I explained what I was doing with the money, she hugged me and said I had saved enough.

LESSON 6: WE DON'T HAVE CONTROL OVER ALL THAT HAPPENS TO US BUT WE HAVE CONTROL OVER HOW WE RESPOND

"Being a mother is the biggest on-the-job training program in existence today!"   **Erma Bombeck**

My mother reminded me, "You have an opportunity most girls don't have. Dad works at the university so you can attend tuition free!" I wanted to attend a college with a garden campus and I wanted to live in a dorm, not commute. My parents told me, "If you give up this chance you will have to work because we have no way to provide your tuition." I chose to work. The problem was that I was not equipped to do anything. My father sent me to an all-academic high school which, at that time, did not even offer typing! I was graduated in January, 1948. I was sixteen years old.

In February 1948, my Dad got me a job at the university. Each morning I stopped at the registrar's office, picked up the handouts the professors left to be copied, then went to all the classes to distribute the handouts. I glanced at each chalkboard and read the questions and answers. I thought, "That is interesting! I wonder what else this class will be studying?" In two weeks I was ready to enroll! Mom said, "Too late. It is the middle of the semester. You must wait till September. By then you may realize how lucky you are!" It took a while but I finally did realize it! I had a great education at Temple University and met my future husband there. At Temple University I trained for my career as a teacher. In responding as I did, I ended up with a wonderful career and a wonderful husband!

With Dad and Mom on the day I graduated from Temple University.

Wedding day: Tom and Margie.

LESSON 7: REMEMBER THINGS YOU LEARNED NOT TO DO!

"Your right hand sustains me."
Psalm 18:35, Holy Bible

At my Dad's insistence, I attended an all-girls high school which offered an academic curriculum only. It was demanding but interesting and I made lifelong friends. My favorite subject was English. When I entered tenth grade my English teacher informed me that I was eligible to take a special course in Creative Writing. I was excited at the prospect. I had always enjoyed writing.

On the first day of Creative Writing I waited eagerly as the teacher shuffled some papers on her desk and finally stood before the class. She handed out sheets of lined paper. Finally she spoke. "You are supposed to be creative. Create!" She returned to her desk and proceeded to do paper work. I, along with the other students, spent the period trying to create a theme and elaborate on it. The teacher never looked up until, when the bell rang she said, "Class dismissed!"

I hoped for some guidance in the ensuing days. It never came. Every day began and ended the same way. After a few weeks I went to the Guidance Counselor for help in removing me from the class. "I am so sorry," the counselor said. "It is too late to put you in another class and you need the credits so you will have to finish the semester in that Creative Writing class." I suffered through the semester. When I started teaching I remembered the many teachers who had a positive influence on me. I also remembered my creative writing teacher and vowed never to use her as a role model!

Girls' High classmates who became lifelong friends. 1st row: Ann; 2nd row: Marie, Diana, Margie, Lydia.

LESSON 8: BE TRUE TO YOURSELF

"Whatever is true, whatever is right, whatever is pure, think about such things." Philippians 4:8

When I was sixteen, one of my close friends had a brother who was three years older than I. Her brother often had his friends over when I happened to be visiting. One of the boys, Joey, and I really liked each other. After we had dated for several months Joey decided that we should get engaged. Joey had never finished high school. He was working in a factory and was satisfied with his job.

I told Joey that I wanted to go to college after I graduated high school. He saw no need for me to do that. Although I really liked Joey very much, I stopped seeing him. It was a wise decision for me.

Margie at 16.

LESSON 9: PEOPLE DO CHANGE THEIR MINDS

"Obstacles are things a person sees when she takes her eyes off the goal."   **Joseph Cossman**

When I first met my husband's mother, she said, "I never thought my son would marry a foreigner." My mother was born in Winsted, Connecticut, my dad in Pittsburgh, Pennsylvania. I was a bit confused. Later I realized that she was shy and my Italian heritage made her uncomfortable. She was English/German. After I married her son, my mother-in-law found great joy at the birth of my children. One day, when my son was a teenager, she asked him what career he would like to pursue. "I think I'd like to be a doctor," he said. Later, when my mother-in-law and I were alone, she said to me, "I thought you loved your son." "I do!" I replied. "Well," she said, "He told me he'd like to be a doctor. Since our family has little money and no connections, you are only setting him up for disappointment if you encourage him."

Our son grew up, went to college, premed, and was ready to apply to medical school. We did not have the money for the first year's tuition. It was the 1960's. His grades were excellent but no help was available because, as the administration explained, "Only money for minorities is available, even for a loan!" Since many medical students did not pass the first year, no loans were available until the second year.

We explained the situation to my husband's parents. Two days later, my father-in-law called. He said, "Tell your son there is money for his first year's tuition. Your mother-in-law is cashing in her Life Insurance policy. She is determined. She insists!" Our son began his medical school education through the kindness and generosity of my mother-in-law. The woman who had not thought it possible, made it happen!

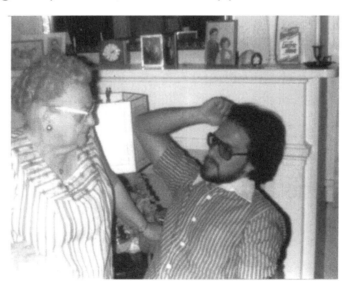

Mother-in-law Ruth and her grandson Jeff.

LESSON 10: KEEP AN OPTIMISTIC ATTITUDE!

"In the middle of any difficulty is opportunity."

Albert Einstein

Though our son was in medical school and our daughter in college, I thought we could manage the tuitions if I had an assistantship at the university where I wanted to earn a doctorate. It was a dream of mine to teach at the college level. I was 53 and decided not to wait any longer. When I approached the department chair, he said there were no openings and no prospects. I asked that my name be on a waiting list. He explained that the current waiting list was overflowing but he finally agreed, reluctantly.

Just two weeks later I got a call to go to the university to interview for an adjunct position. I was amazed and asked the administrator why there was an opening suddenly and why I, being so far down on the waiting list, was invited to be interviewed. He said, quite candidly, "The professor who wants an intern is very demanding. In fact, she is so demanding that interns have always quit after two weeks! You are mature. I think you will last!" I called my mother and explained the situation. She said, "Go for it! It is a position you want some day so it will be good experience. I doubt that she will ask you to do anything that is immoral, illegal or fattening!" I got the job and stayed three years until I received my doctor's degree.

The professor spent her time doing research for promotion. I did all the planning, teaching and evaluating. Although she was very demanding, she never did ask me to do anything illegal, immoral or fattening! I did get valuable experience and a great recommendation from her when I left!

Margie receives a doctorate in education from Rutgers University; her mother beams with pride.

LESSON 11: CHILDREN LEARN BY EXAMPLE AND BY PRACTICING WHAT THEY HAVE LEARNED

"Plant in children what you wish to put into the life of our time." Lucy Wheelock

As a first grade teacher I was concerned that the majority of my students did not engage in creative thinking. They saw no alternatives to a situation when things did not go as planned. Children got upset when a crayon broke! I decided to teach creative thinking. The next time a crayon broke I stopped the lesson. "Now, what can John do about this?" I asked. Answers were versions of "Throw the picture away," and "Stop drawing." I posed some questions. "What other color can he use for this drawing?" "What else can he draw that would fit the picture?"

Soon the children adopted the philosophy and amazed me with their inventiveness! The next time crayons broke, when students forgot their lunches from home, or it rained when we planned to play outside, the children were quick to respond with, "Draw another picture!" "Call your mother to bring your lunch or buy lunch and tell the lunch lady you will pay her tomorrow!" "We can play inside with our board games!"

LESSON 12: AVANTI! GO FORWARD!

"Do not conform to the pattern of this world, but be transformed by the renewing of your mind."
Romans 12:2

I returned to teaching after my two children were in school fulltime. I loved first grade and was happy to be working although the class was a real challenge. The principal kept adding to my enrollment with children who had special needs. My class soon had the largest number of students and the largest number of children with behavior problems. When I questioned him, the principal replied, "You have the most success with these children so I naturally put them in your room!" My class was supposed to be heterogeneous and not special education. I felt gratified at being able to help the children in my class although it was not an ideal situation.

One day I walked into the principal's office and announced my intention to resign at the end of the current school year. "You cannot resign!" he said. "You are needed here! What do you think you should be doing?" "I think I should be following my own mind," I replied. "I am going to attend graduate school and get a master's degree in school counseling." And I did. For several years I was a school counselor.

Then, once again, my heart found a new direction. The superintendent of schools asked me to train student teachers during their practicum. I found such joy in it that I decided to enroll as a doctoral student in order to someday teach college students as a college faculty member. I received a doctorate in Education and taught at the university level with a great sense of fulfillment.

Margie with her students.

LESSON 13: WHAT WE REALLY, REALLY WANTED!

"There will be showers of blessing."

Ezekiel 34:26

When I was pregnant with our first child, my husband and I assured each other that the gender of our baby did not matter. We wished only that our child be healthy. We meant it! We prayed for a healthy baby. Fortunately, the nine months went by with no problem as we eagerly bought furniture and other necessities. There were baby showers and preparations galore. My due date passed and the baby did not arrive but two weeks later I felt the baby coming.

The labor was long but eventually it was time for the baby to come. In 1954, it was common for expectant mothers to have injections to ease the pain of delivery. I had them. That meant I was unaware of the process! My husband was by my side waiting for the delivery. When I finally awoke I asked him, "Did I have the baby?" he said, "Yes." "Is it healthy?" I wanted to know. He said, "Yes." I thanked the Lord for my healthy baby. My next question was, "What do we have?" he smiled and said, "What we really, really wanted!" "It's a girl!" I exclaimed. "No, it's a boy!" he said. To this day, 60 years later, we still laugh about this. The thrill is that our son Jeff has always been and continues to be a great source of joy. God gave us a wonderful son. Six years after our son was born we were blessed with a wonderful baby girl. Fifty-four years later daughter Karen continues to be a great blessing! We have been truly blessed with what we really, really wanted!

Be grateful when you receive what you really want!

Karen Louise and Jeffrey Thomas.

LESSON 14: MAKE THE BEST OF THE SITUATION!

"Rejoice that your name is written in heaven."
Luke 10:20

In the United States in the 1930's and 1940's, public school teachers were paid low salaries. The country was trying to recover from the Depression. One young man I know really enjoyed working with children. He wanted to be a teacher. His parents wanted the best for him and were afraid that it would be very difficult for him to raise a family on a teacher's salary. He was engaged to be married and did look forward to raising a family. His parents convinced him to study engineering. He did. He married, had a family and got a job which paid a salary that afforded him a beautiful home and in which he raised children for whom he provided a college education.

After many years he retired. One day the principal of the elementary school his children had attended called to ask his help to volunteer. Tutors were needed and the school budget could not provide paid tutors for all the children who could benefit from tutoring. The man responded. He loved it. To this day, he is tutoring and enjoying every minute of it!

LESSON 15: ALLOW LOVE TO PREVAIL

"May your unfailing love be my comfort."

Psalm 119:76

In 1890, when she was sixteen, Carolina was told she would marry Tullio, a man twenty years older than she. He had a small grocery store and was able to support a wife and children. Carolina's parents had five daughters and they believed their responsibility was to see that all of them had husbands to take care of them. Carolina was 5'9" tall. Tullio was 4'11". They were married in 1906.

Although Carolina was not in love with Tullio she followed her father's orders. She had five children. Her first child, Carl, was a very bright boy. She told him that if he went to work and gave her all his earnings she would save them for college where he could meet a rich girl who was going to have a profession like Carl was destined to have. Carl worked in a soup factory and gave all his salary to his mother.

When Carl was sixteen he met Margaret, a girl whose parents had been friends and neighbors of Carl's parents in Italy. They fell in love. Margaret's parents were not rich. Margaret worked in a sewing factory with no hope of going to college. Carolina told Carl to stop seeing Margaret.

When Carl said he planned to marry Margaret, Carolina said, "If you do, I will keep all the money saved for your college tuition and you will no longer be my son. Margaret is poorer than we are. We did not come to America to stay poor." Carl continued to work and give his wages to his mother. He also continued to date Margaret. Their dates were walks on Broad Street in South Philadelphia near where they both lived. Carl hoped that his mother would change her mind about Margaret.

One day, four years later, when Carl and Margaret were both twenty years old, Carl approached his mother. Carolina had not changed her mind. In fact, she told Carl she and Tullio were moving their family to Pittsburgh and wanted Carl to go with them, without Margaret. Carl walked out of the house and went to see Margaret. He told Margaret they were getting married that day. They took a train to Media, Pennsylvania, and got married by a Justice of the Peace. When they returned, they went to live with Giovanna, Margaret's mother. Margaret worked in a factory as a seamstress and sent Carl to college. Carl became a Pharmacist. They raised a family and their love lasted until Carl died at age 58. This is a true story of my mother and father. After living her whole life in a forced and loveless marriage, Carolina could not bring herself to support her son's marriage with a loving spouse. How sad.

Dad, Mom, Margie, sister Carol, brother Bob.

LESSON 16: IT CAN BE A JOY TO LOVE ALL CREATURES

"The power that a woman has is to help people grow in the right way, with love and warmth."
Maria Schell

Growing up, I never had a pet. My mother loved people, especially children. She was kind and caring to humans. She was afraid of animals, all kinds and all sizes. I grew up very uncomfortable around animals. My husband Tom's family had a puppy when he was a child and he would have liked having a dog but was considerate of my insecurity because, as he acknowledged, most of the responsibility would be mine, since the children were at school and he was at work.

When our son Jeff was ten years old the television show LASSIE was very popular. We all enjoyed the show, particularly Jeff and our daughter Karen, four years old at the time. One morning, before he left for school, Jeff said, "I had a dog dream last night." I asked him to explain. Jeff said, "I dreamed that Lassie was living with us." I told him I understood because I knew he liked dogs and we had just watched the show. After that incident however, Jeff reported that he had many "dog dreams," even on nights when the show was not aired! The "dog dreams" went on and on. Finally, after much soul searching, I decided that our family should get a dog.

Having a dog was not easy for me. It took several weeks before I was comfortable with Taffy. Tom was right. Much of the responsibility was mine. I grew to love Taffy. When I had a good day, it was a bonus to have Taffy welcome me so warmly when I returned from work. On bad days, it was a great stress reducer to walk Taffy!

No one was sadder than I when, fourteen years later, our beloved pet had to be put to sleep. Yes, love can mean more than loving people.

Jeff's dog Taffy.

LESSON 17: EVERY NAME HAS A STORY BEHIND IT!

"There isn't anyone you couldn't love once you hear their story." **Mary Lou Kownacki**

In the early nineteen hundreds, immigrants could not enter the United States unless they had a promise of employment. Corporations went overseas and offered to pay the passage to America if people would sign that they would work for the company who was paying their passage to America. My mother's parents, Giovanna and Vincenzo Borrelli, came here as teenagers. My mother was born in America. The factory closed and the Borrelli couple was deported back to Italy. Years later another company offered them passage and they returned. My mother was then five years old. At Ellis Island the customs officer asked what their little girl's name was. My grandmother said, "Michela." The customs officer replied, "That sounds like Michael! You are in America now. She needs an American name. Her name is Margaret."

When I was seven years old I complained that my name was too long. Because I could not fit Margaret Jeannette Malamisuro on one line, I was failing handwriting. My grandmother said, "That isn't really your name anyway." She told me the story about "Michela." I asked her why she did not resist the suggestion made by the customs officer. She answered, "I was afraid he would have me deported!" My mother remained "Margaret." My father wanted me named after my mother.

A customs officer at Ellis Island is responsible for naming me!

What is the story behind your name?

Grandfather
Vincenzo Borrelli.

Grandmom Giovanna, Jeff, Margie, Mom.

LESSON 18: WORK HARD AND TRUST GOD!

"The best way to find yourself is to lose yourself in the service of others." **Mahatma Gandhi**

A friend called to ask me, "May I pick you up next Monday and take you to speak at City Team?"

I had just published my third book, *AVANTI! Tales of Love and Survival*, and had begun speaking to groups about overcoming life's obstacles. However, I did not know if my presentation would help a group who was homeless, on parole and out of work. "Just tell your personal story and a few stories from your book," Sandy suggested. I prayed about it and finally agreed. I worked hard on choosing stories I thought might relate to the group.

On the day of my talk, I felt calm but not very confident. The group did seem to relate to the stories of my years growing up poor in South Philadelphia and other stories of how our family overcame their disadvantages. I quoted my beloved Grandmother Giovanna, "Work hard and trust God!" After the talk, the group shared their comments with me. "Good talk! It was just what they needed to hear!" Each person was referring to all of the others in the group! They were all saying that EVERYONE ELSE needed to hear what I said. They said, "They all got your message!" I asked what they thought the message was. They all shouted, "Never give up!" I had not used that phrase though that was my underlying message. I thanked them all for listening and I thanked God for the response. I learned that Grandmother Giovanna was right. "Work hard and trust God!"

LESSON 19: A FAMILY LEGACY

"Make a joyful noise all ye lands. Be thankful unto Him and bless His name, for the Lord is good. His mercy is everlasting." **Psalm 66**

I awoke one morning with chest pain. Having had digestive problems since childhood, chest pain was nothing new. This pain however reminded me of the experience my father had. He also had digestive problems and, as my mother related to me, considered the pain another digestive problem. When the pain persisted my mother called an ambulance. My father died of a heart attack, in the ambulance, on the way to the hospital. I told my husband to take me to the hospital. When he asked me why, I replied. "I'd rather go to the hospital and have it be nothing than to stay home and have it be something. The pain reminds me of what happened to my father." My husband took me to the hospital where I was diagnosed as having a heart attack.

My Dad was my role model. He loved to read. So do I. He did crossword puzzles regularly. So do I. He believed that people who are different are not wrong for being different and should be respected for their uniqueness. I believe that also. He loved children and enjoyed teaching. So do I.

There are many legacies I inherited from my dad. I feel that the most recent one was a call to go to the hospital with the chest pain. I thank God for my earthly father.

My parents.

LESSON 20: KEEP THE FAITH!

"Serve the Lord with gladness. It is He that hath made us and not we ourselves. Be thankful to Him and bless His name." **Psalm 100**

Several years ago I was diagnosed with dry Macular Degeneration. Recently I was told it had progressed to wet Macular Degeneration. Injections have helped at times but the prognosis is poor. I was told that there is no cure and that my vision will keep diminishing.

At my last checkup, the retina specialist exclaimed, "This is amazing! You have had macular degeneration for twenty years and you are in your eighties. I do not understand how you can see anything. You are writing books! What are you doing for your eyes?" I answered, "Spinach and prayer." The doctor replied, "I am a scientist." My response was, "Doctor, you asked me a question and I gave you a truthful answer." "Well," said the doctor, "keep doing what you are doing." I said, "Doctor, I fully intend to!"

LESSON 21: LEARN TO RECOVER FROM A NATIONAL DISASTER

"The lord preserves the faithful."   **Psalm 31:23**

All my life I dreamed of visiting the Italian village of my ancestors. My father's and my mother's parents were friends and neighbors in Montaguto, Southern Italy. None of the grandparents ever had an opportunity to revisit and my parents never got an opportunity to visit. On my 70th birthday my children announced a "roots trip" for me and, "by virtue of his position as my spouse," my husband was to accompany me. I was thrilled! After many failed attempts at trying to locate Montaguto, I wondered if I would ever locate the village. Embassies told me the village never existed. When I persisted, I was told that if it ever existed, I had the wrong spelling, or the village was destroyed in an earthquake.

One day, when my husband and I were in Borders bookstore, Tom asked me, "Is this the town you've been looking for?" He pointed to a spot on a map of Italy he had found on a shelf. There it was, spelled exactly as I had been told by my grandmother Giovanna! The next step was to make contact with any relative living there. After much searching I found a woman who spoke fluent Italian and understood the dialect from the region. She said, "Every Italian village has two things, a church and a bakery. Tell me your maiden name and your mother's maiden name." I did. She called me a few weeks later. "I found a cousin of yours living in Montaguto. Tell me what you want to say and I will write to him." She wrote to the church.

The letter was delivered and I got a reply, in Italian of course. Translated, it said that he, Antonio, was very happy to hear from me and to know that a relative in America was interested in making contact with him!

The trip was amazing. I asked Tom to take photos of me all during the visit. He said, "You never want your picture taken." I told him that if I didn't have photos of me in Montaguto I'll think I dreamed the whole trip! We stayed at the small hotel in Montaguto, toured the village and visited Antonio and his family. We left Montaguto on our return trip home by going to Lecce, then to Naples and Gallipoli, where we heard that there had been a terrible airplane crash in the United States. We continued on to Brussels, Belgium, to discover our flight home was cancelled.

The newspaper headlines screamed ACCIDENTE! I thought that there must have been a really tremendous accident to cause such a ruckus! Worse news came soon. NO ACCIDENTE! TERRORISTA! It was September 11, 2001. As unbelievable as it seemed, it was real. My immediate reaction was that I may never see my family again. Tom and I stayed in Brussels for a few days before we could book a flight back to the United States. I prayed that the terroristic threat, which had caused such a tremendous loss of lives already, was over. When our plane landed at the airport in Newark, NJ, I thanked God.

It is now December 2014. Tom and I just returned from a trip to the 9/11 memorial museum in New York City. I shed tears for the 3000 people who perished and prayed the disaster would never recur.

LESSON 22: USE THE TALENT YOU DO HAVE!

"Your best is enough!"   **Tony Horton**

Growing up I was frustrated because I was not coordinated. I could not play tennis, golf or softball. The easiest thing for me seemed to be talking! I liked to give presentations. When I became a teacher and seminar leader, I found my passion. I continued presenting talks.

When our granddaughter Jenny had a baby boy, Chase, I was thrilled at being a great-grandmother. On December 5, 2013, I had a heart attack. Chase was then exactly four months old. While I was in the hospital, Jenny brought Chase to see me. Jenny was told that children had to be 14 years old to be visitors. She protested, saying that she knew Chase's appearance would enhance my recovery. She was right of course but could not get permission. The rule would be upheld.

My daughter Karen, the new grandmother, had an idea. While some of the family gathered around Jenny and Chase, others gathered around me. Karen came to my room with a smart phone. She called Jenny to put her smart phone near Chase so I could see him. When I saw him I started talking to him.

Great-grandson Chase.

When I paused, Chase started talking to me! We kept that up for a few minutes until I exclaimed, "Chase is talking to me!" The family replied, "Impossible! At four months he is not yet talking!" Chase and I continued. He was jibber-jabbering with proper inflection, though it was not in English. Finally, Johnny, 27 year old grandson, shouted, "Everybody be quiet! I heard him! Chase was talking to Grandma Margie! He obviously inherited her talking gene!" When I got home from the hospital and visited the Lanes, Jenny said, "Grandma, Chase does not talk with people like he does with you!" You are the only one he has conversations with!

My talking talent has helped me to be active in my retirement community and to continue to serve. When my husband Tom and I moved into a continuing care community, he cautioned me about venturing out of the apartment alone. I have no sense of direction. Tom was afraid I would get lost easily. On the second day Tom noticed a sign, "Tours are us!" and encouraged me to call for a guide. I did.

After about fifteen minutes, the guide asked, "Would you like to tour the TV Studio?" I answered, "Sure! I have never done that. It sounds interesting."

The guide opened the door. She stepped in. I stepped in. She said, "What do you think?" "I am ready," I said. "Ready?" she replied. "This is it. There is a sofa, a chair and a camera." To this day, I do not remember what I said next. All I know is that the producer ran to me and exclaimed, "You are now a TV Host! I can tell you have a talent for talking!" I protested, "I just moved in and I do not know what a TV Host is responsible for." The producer said, "Go home and check your e mail. Look at the program schedule and times for the coming week. Let me know what programs interest you and what times you are available!"

Tom and I have lived at Maris Grove for three years now. I just filmed my forty-first interview show. I believe I might have a talent for talking. I thank God for the opportunities to do so!

Chase will certainly grow up to have many talents, but I hope he will honor his "talking gene" among them. Whatever our talents, they give us important ways to find satisfaction and to serve.

LESSON 23: EXPERIENCE IS THE BEST TEACHER

"It's not what you look at that matters, it's what you see." **Henry David Thoreau**

Shortly after I moved to Maris Grove a neighbor told me she was expecting her daughter and son-in-law to visit her that day. "Great!" I replied. "Not so great," she said. My son-in-law is coming very reluctantly. He is a builder and he is afraid I will try to talk him into moving here. He said that he wants to die in the home he built." I asked her if she planned to encourage him to move to Maris Grove. "No," she said, "I just want him to see where I live."

The next day I saw that neighbor again. "Did your daughter and son-in-law visit you?" I asked. "Yes and the strangest thing happened! He was not here even a half hour when he looked at me and said, 'Mom, how old do you have to be to be allowed to move here?'" I asked her what her response was. She said, "I told him I thought he had no interest in moving here. He said that was before he saw the place!"

LESSON 24: AVANTI! FROM PEGGY TO DR.G.

"Unless you try to do something beyond what you have already mastered, you will never grow."
Ralph Waldo Emerson

"Why would you worry about sending Peggy to college? She's a girl! She'll get married and have children. For that she needs a college education?" I was a high school senior and had been in my bedroom studying. I came downstairs for a snack and overheard our next door neighbor talking to my Dad. My Dad answered, "Peggy is very smart in school. She deserves a chance to be whatever she wants to be." The neighbor insisted, "It's a waste!" My Dad replied, "No it isn't. She is my daughter. I am going to see that she can go to college if she wants."

It was 1947. It was not unusual for the working class to think as our neighbor did. My mother worked in a factory sewing men's shirts to earn money for Dad's college tuition. After Dad graduated from Pharmacy School, he was offered a job in a Pharmacy. He chose instead to work at the Temple Hospital Pharmacy so I could go to Temple University tuition free. I graduated from Temple University and began teaching. After I married and had children I stopped working until my children were in school. When I resumed teaching I discovered I had a special interest in helping children with special needs and, after getting a Master's degree, became a school counselor. When the superintendent continually sent me college students to train, I left school counseling, earned a doctorate and taught at the college level until I retired. Thanks to my Dad, I became what I wanted to be! I was able to teach AND be a mom!

Envoi

This book is dedicated to all those who follow the AVANTI! ROAD. It is the way of confidence that, with God's help, you can move forward! AVANTI!

Margaret Mayo Gibson was born and raised in South Philadelphia. She was educated at the Philadelphia High School for Girls, Temple University, the College of New Jersey, and Rutgers University. During Dr. Gibson's career, she served as a classroom teacher, school counselor, child development specialist, assistant professor at Rutgers University and West Chester University, and parenting consultant.

Dr. Gibson is the author of parenting articles, devotionals, and the books *A Seed in Good Soil, Parenting through Childhood Memories*; *Family Treasures, A Guide to Writing Your Life Stories*; and *Avanti! Tales of Love and Survival*. Dr. Gibson and her husband, Thomas M. Gibson, live in Glen Mills, Pennsylvania.

1st row: Jenny Dickinson, Donna Gibson, Jeff Gibson, Karen Dickinson, John Dickinson; 2nd row: Jeff Lane, Brad Gibson, Greg Gibson, Johnny Dickinson; 3rd row: Tom Gibson, Margie Gibson.

.

18615804R00031

Made in the USA
San Bernardino, CA
21 January 2015